the drawings of

Leonardo da Vinci

Introduction by

ELMER BELT, M.D.

BORDEN PUBLISHING COMPANY

FIRST EDITION

Library of Congress Catalog Card Number: 62-19992

PRINTED IN THE UNITED STATES OF AMERICA

LEONARDO DA VINCI

1452-1519

In the mind of leonardo we encounter a great phenomenon, an accomplishment which nature seldom, if ever, has reduplicated. Nature gave to Leonardo an original inventive mind of superlative penetration and depth of comprehension.

Leonardo was illegitimate, the result of an early passionate love affair of his father, the young, highly intelligent notary, Ser Piero d'Antonio of Vinci, with a country girl from the nearby farming area of Anciano. In Leonardo's education, because of his illegitimacy, fortune favored him. He was not subjected to the sterile scholastic education of his day but, instead, became in his own words "a disciple of experience." His insatiable curiosity led him to seek out all the secrets of nature. He became a master of correct and disciplined observation. Wise analyses of his keen observations of nature followed by experiments leading to new observations, made of Leonardo one of the greatest discoverers of all times.

Early in life, Leonardo developed a draftsmanship which was effortless and perfectly accurate. This quality combined with constant, careful note-taking, which reinforced the accuracy of his unusual memory, gave him a well-stocked mind which he used clearly and effectively in every realm of thought.

Leonardo was much more interested in the thrill of discovery than in the drudgery of compiling. His unedited notebook manuscripts grew into a loosely organized encyclopedic mass of material. These written notes have the freshness as well as the incompleteness of observations just jotted down. They contain Leonardo's terse reflections upon everything within his wide purview and, since their publication, they have become the best known laboratory notes in the world. Onto these sheets went Leonardo's drawings of flowers, of human figures, of distant mountains. Strong and convincing, his use of half light and strong shadows imparted a living quality even to his merest quick sketches. Here in his notebooks are hundreds of drawings by means of which Leonardo worked out and stored up ideas and memories of fleeting forms for future paintings. Here are images from the whole of nature dropped onto these pages with the finest coordination of hand and eye in the history of European art. Their total number is larger than that of any artist of the fifteenth century. The drawings are accompanied by precisely written conclusions encompassing scientific statements in the realms of what we now term botany, geology, minerology, astronomy and comparative anatomy. These notes reveal an intense hunger for knowledge in all fields. Here, in the realm of art, are experiments in perspective, on light from all heights and distances, the effect of dust in atmosphere and what it does to perspective. The experiments in the effect of color upon the eye are described and Leonardo, in studying the texture of feathers, as he goes to nature for help in the construction of his flying machine, discovers that the mesh of the feather when held between his eye and the sun splits the light into rainbow hues. He promptly created a screen of wire which produced the same effect. Thus he became the first to discover that white light is made up of a combination of colored rays. He applies this discovery immediately as a solution to the appearance of color in the reflected light from bird feathers, the color of which he was unable to wash out of the feather with any solution at hand. Among these notes are myriads of such observations and discoveries.

The flowering period of the Renaissance was from 1450 to 1520. Leonardo's birth year was 1452. He died 67 years later in 1519. Thus Leonardo's life spans the brightest period of the Renaissance and of this period he was the supreme flower. Leonardo was born in the foothills of Monte Albano at the hill town village of Vinci which lies in a fold of the Apennines along the course of the Arno about half way between Florence and Pisa. His father, noting his artistic gift, apprenticed him to Andrea del Verrocchio (he of the true eye). In Verrocchio's studio at the Via del Agnolo, in Florence, Leonardo brushed minds with the greatest artists of the day. This training with Verrocchio was to be his entire formal education. As a result of his training under Verrocchio and of the contacts made during his training period his educational roots were deep in the middle ages but due to his original mind he became the outstanding herald of the modern world.

\ Leonardo was a scientist, passionately devoted to art, a realistic student of nature and yet a dreamy idealist. As a student he proved to be gifted in every field of science and of art. He excelled in drawing, in clay modeling, in mechanical draftsmanship and in every artistic endeavor. He was admitted to the guild of painters at the age of twenty. By twenty-five he was famous.\

Writing today, Andre Chastel* states, "It is surprising how few pictures he painted, particularly after his fortieth year, and this has been remarked on ever since the sixteenth century. Equally surprising is how soon and how assiduously his works were copied, so that one has the feeling that whatever he did produce was observed and made use of with disturbing persistence. The naïveté of the myth, which made him a high priest who was something of a necromancer, a sage who could satisfy every expectation, and a technician who could perform any feat, whether it was in hydraulics or military machines, is actually less remarkable than the servility and veneration which obviously surrounded him and which assured his every whim as well as his major discoveries the same applause nowadays accorded to the least act of Matisse or Picasso."

Into every one of Leonardo's paintings went the rich background of experience seen in his accumulated drawings. Each painting became a work of great beauty mirroring the wonders of nature and into each came life through the vigor of Leonardo's execution and fidelity to nature.

Leonardo's drawings which were at first a scaffolding, by the aid of which his paintings were produced, were later extended to become part of the paraphernalia of scientific research. Even as such they never become diagrammatic. Each drawing reflects Leonardo's extraordinary feeling for the beauty of line and texture.

Like the expanding waves set up by a pebble thrown into a still pool, so well described by Leonardo, the force of Leonardo's thought spread widely, losing none of its power as it moved on through the centuries, ever surprising new generations of thinkers with its beauty, leading them to expressions of praise for him and to a greater love and understanding of the beautiful.

At the time of the High Renaissance the advent of printing as a means of communicating ideas, the perfection of the convention of perspective and illustration, and the awakening of scholarly interest in the great accomplishments of earlier civilizations all converge to a focus as Leonardo attained maturity. The brilliant light which they brought to man's intellectual life burns most brightly in Leonardo's own environment. Leonardo's special ability to absorb new ideas, his great talent in self-expression, both in words and in the graphic arts, and his awareness that of all the impressions experienced by man it is his own personal experiences that count most, soon made Leonardo master of his environment. His record of what he felt and saw remains for us a forceful expression of the impact upon an unusually bright mind of the experience of living in the stimulating atmosphere of his own day.

This window Leonardo opens for us upon the Italian Renaissance is especially important since we may there mark the inception of our own age. We can better understand the meaning of civilization today if we understand Leonardo and his age and its essential difference from the ages that preceded it. In Leonardo and his brilliant contemporaries we find masters of their environment instead of slaves to it. They were unhampered by tradition. They lifted themselves above it. They made their new philosophy of the study of nature and its forces the popular pursuit of their day and thus made the bright path of intellectual freedom easier for us. Through them we have gained the desire and the power to observe natural phenomena, becoming ourselves "disciples of experience" as was Leonardo.

In following them toward an understanding and control of the forces of nature in our environment we have steadily made life more beautiful, more healthful and more rewarding for all mankind. If we are able to continue following the lead which the Renaissance has given us, man may rise to heights as yet undreamed of.

Elmer Belt, M.D.

*The Genius of Leonardo Da Vinci, by Andre Chastel, 1961, The Orion Press Inc., New York

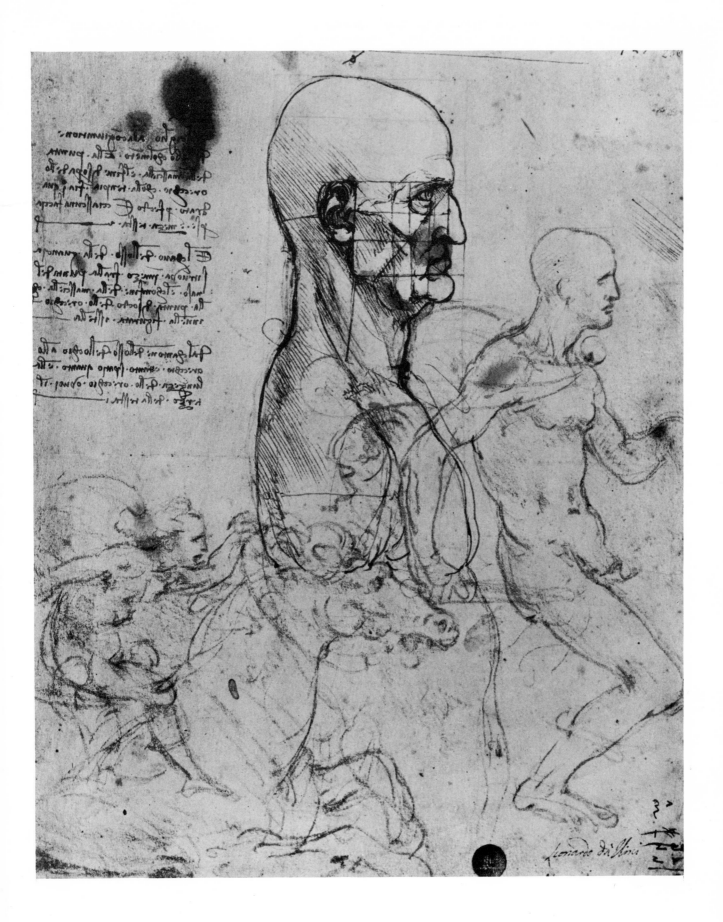

Profile of a Man and Studies of Horsemen
Pen and ink
ACADEMY, VENICE, ITALY

Studies of Horses and of Horses' Heads

Silver-point on buff prepared surface

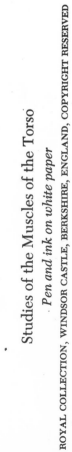

Studies of the Muscles of the Torso

Pen and ink on white paper

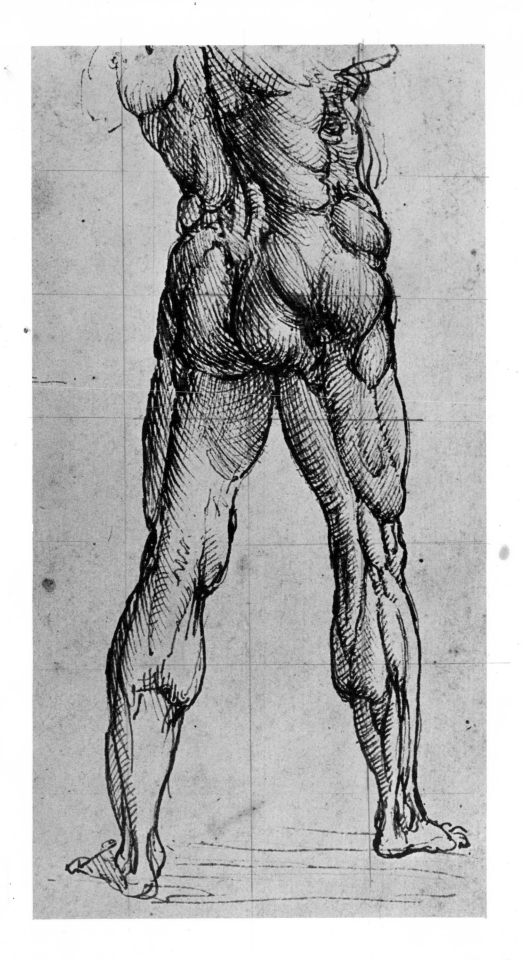

Muscle Study of Figure from Rear

Pen and ink

ROYAL LIBRARY, TURIN, ITALY

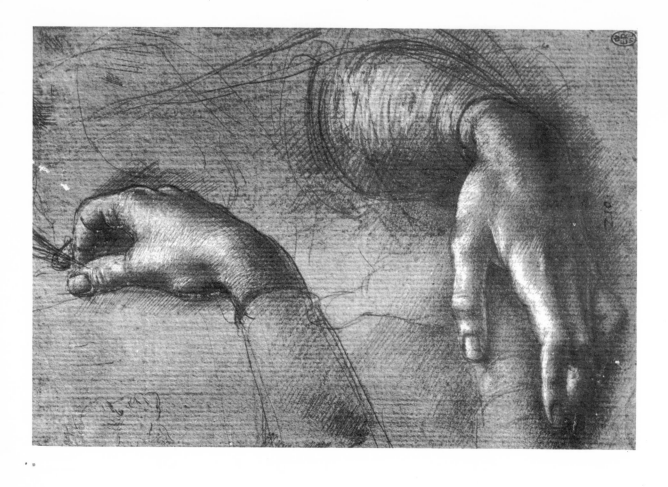

Study of a Woman's Hands
Silver-point on pink prepared surface

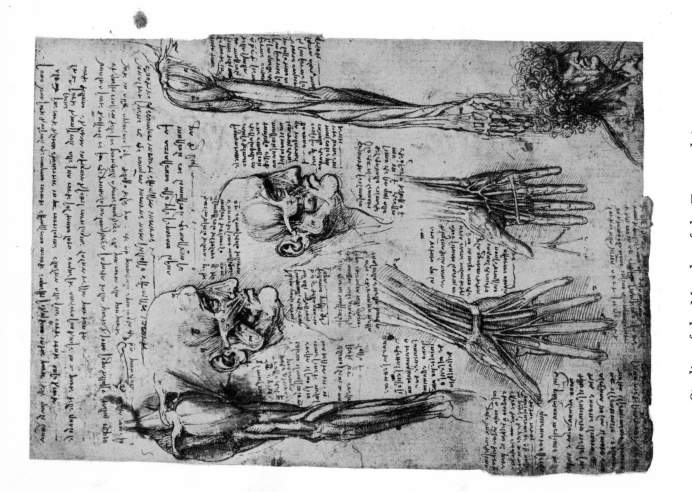

Studies of the Muscles of the Face and Arm
Pen and ink over faint black chalk on white paper

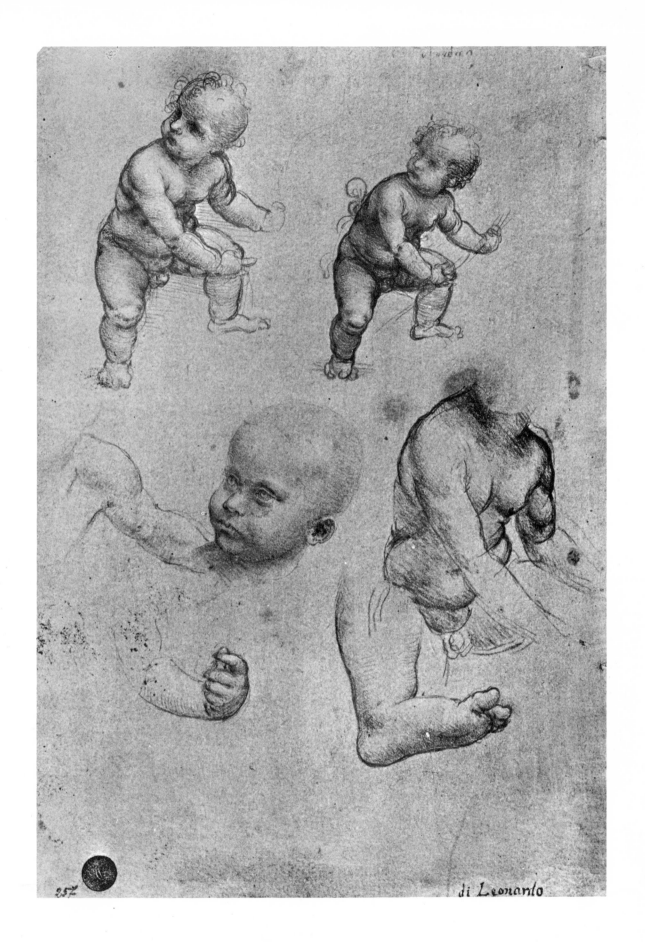

Studies of a Child

Red chalk

ACADEMY, VENICE, ITALY

Study of the Head of a Man Shouting

Black and red chalk

MUSEUM OF FINE ARTS, BUDAPEST, HUNGARY

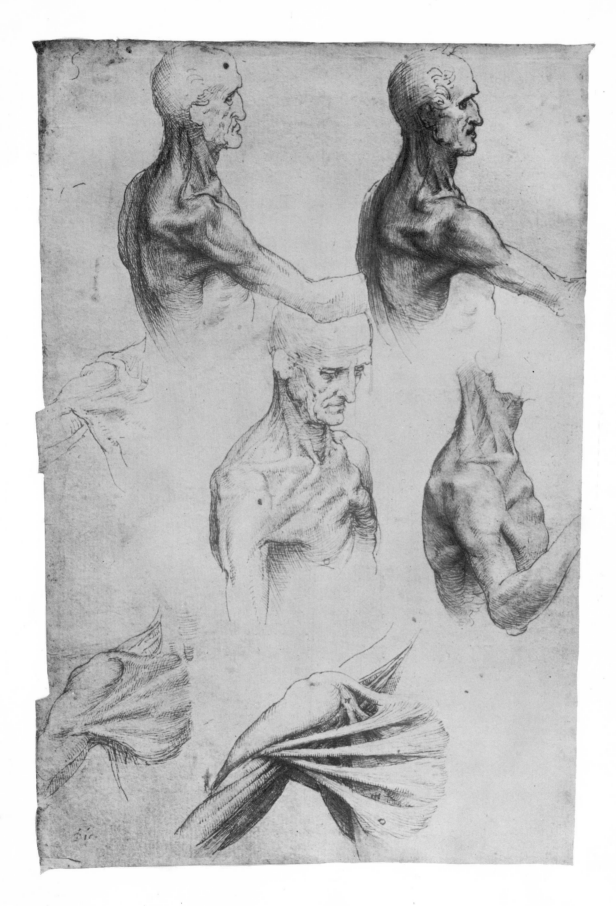

Studies of the Head and Shoulders of a Man

Pen and ink

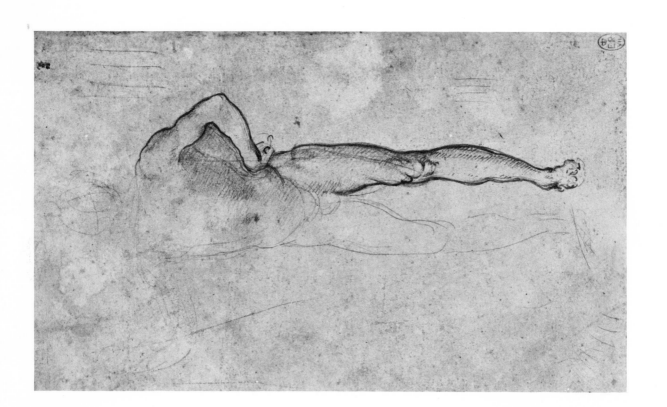

Study for a Youthful St. John The Baptist
Silver-point on blue prepared surface

Study of a Nude Man
Silver-point on blue prepared surface

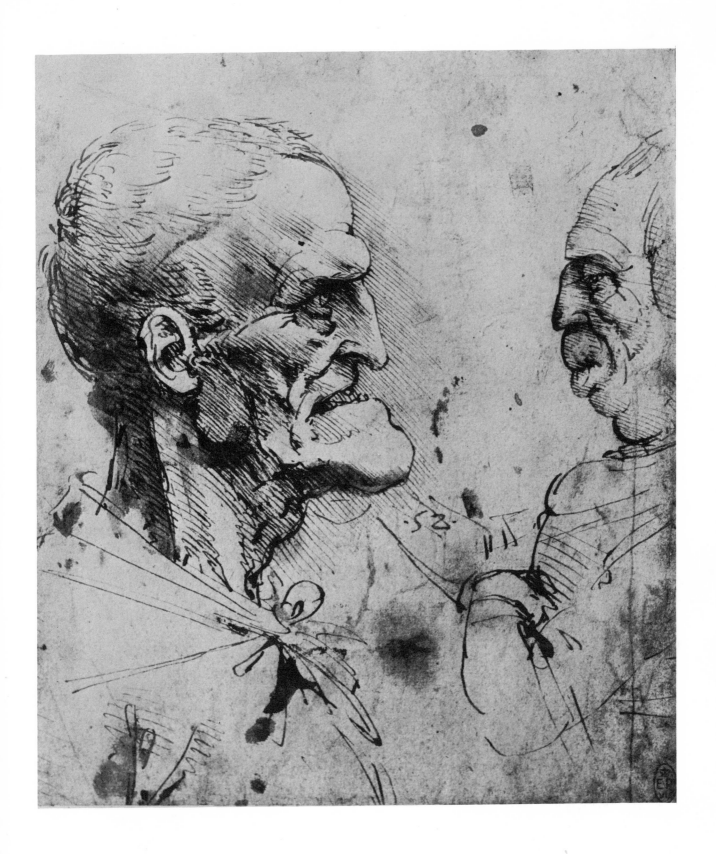

Grotesque Profiles of a Man and Woman Facing

Pen and ink and wash

Studies of the Head of Cesare Borgia
Red chalk
ROYAL LIBRARY, TURIN, ITALY

A Horseman Trampling on a Fallen Foe
Silver-point on blue prepared surface
ROYAL COLLECTION, WINDSOR CASTLE, BERKSHIRE, ENGLAND, COPYRIGHT RESERVED

The Madonna and Child and Other Studies

Pen and ink

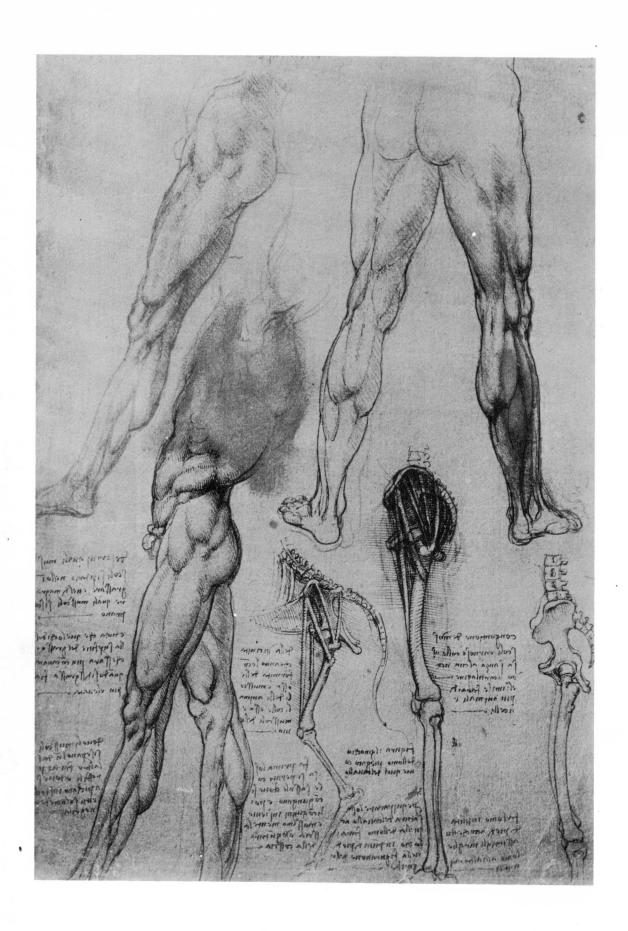

Studies of Human Legs and Bones of Leg in a Man and in a Dog

Pen and ink over red chalk

Profile of an Old Bearded Man

Black chalk on coarse gray paper

Self-Portrait of Leonardo
Red chalk
ROYAL LIBRARY, TURIN, ITALY

Virgin and Child with St. Anne and Infant St. John

Cartoon in charcoal on brown paper

ROYAL ACADEMY OF ARTS, LONDON, ENGLAND

Five Grotesque Heads
Pen and ink
ROYAL COLLECTION, WINDSOR CASTLE, BERKSHIRE, ENGLAND, COPYRIGHT RESERVED

Studies of an Angel, of Horsemen and Other Figures

Pen and ink and black chalk

Two Studies of the Upper Part of an Old Man and Studies of Arms
Pen and ink

Two Horse Studies
Silver-point on pale pinkish-buff prepared surface

Profile of a Warrior Wearing an Elaborate Helmet

Silver-point on cream-colored prepared surface

BRITISH MUSEUM, LONDON, ENGLAND

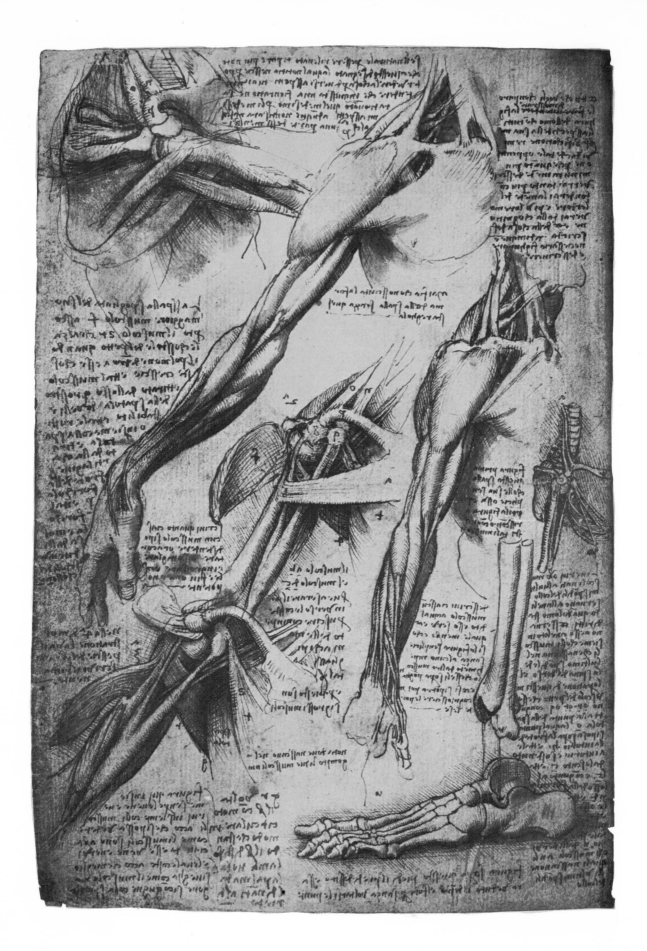

Studies of the Chest and Right Arm of Man

Pen and ink over faint-black chalk on white paper

Study of the Drapery of a Figure Kneeling
Drawn with brush on blue prepared paper

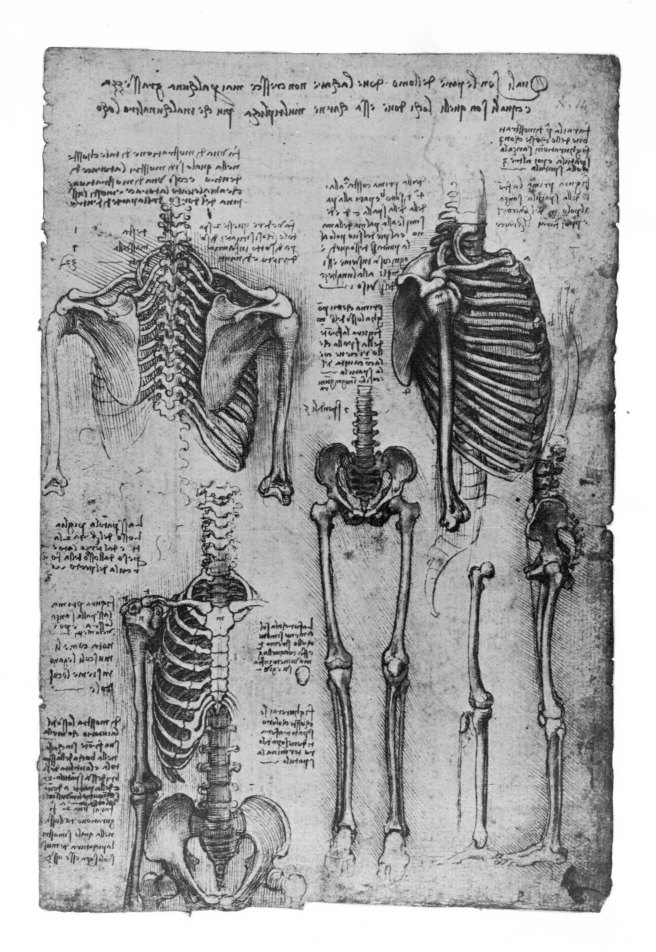

Anatomical Studies

Pen and ink over faint-black chalk

Studies of Figure and Putti for an Adoration

Pen and ink over metal-point

Study of the Lower Half of a Nude Man

Black chalk

Studies of a Woman's Head and Bust

Silver-point on pink prepared surface

Studies of Nude Soldiers with Swords

Pen and ink

ROYAL LIBRARY, TURIN, ITALY

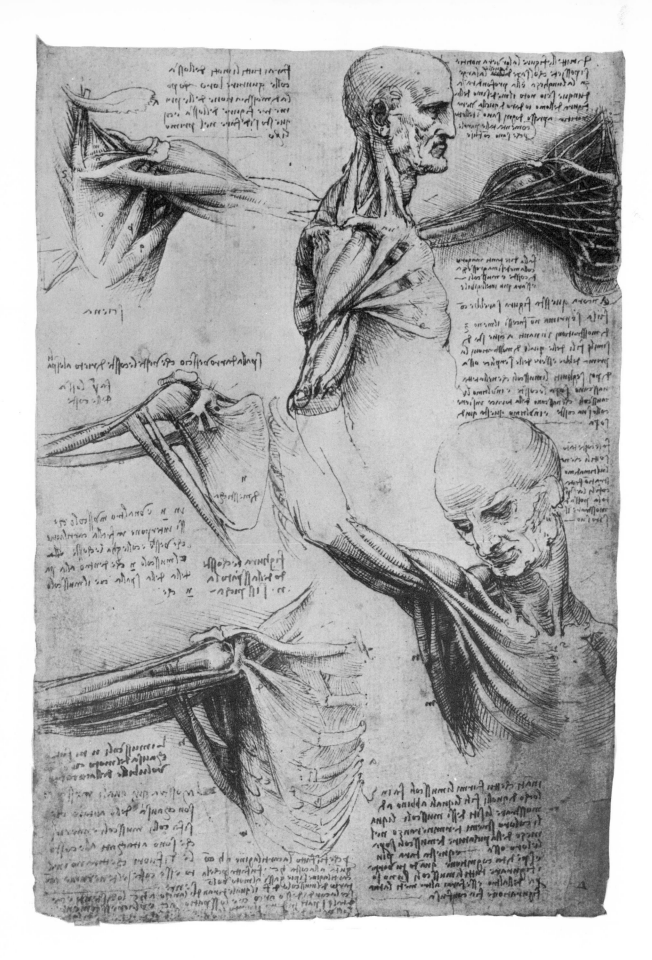

Anatomical Studies of a Man's Neck and Shoulders

Pen and ink

St. Jerome

Silver-point, heightened with white

ROYAL COLLECTION, WINDSOR CASTLE, BERKSHIRE, ENGLAND, COPYRIGHT RESERVED

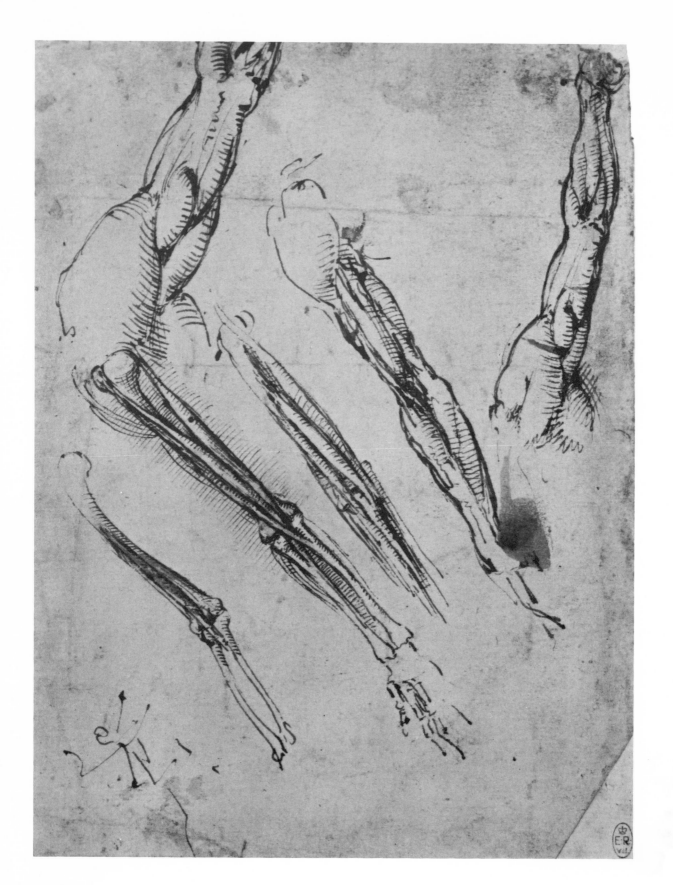

Six Studies of an Arm

Pen and ink

Study of Drapery of a Woman Kneeling
Silver-point on red prepared surface
CORSINI GALLERY, ROME, ITALY

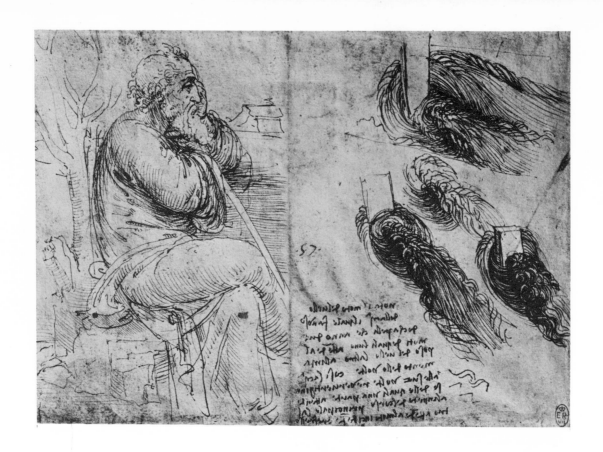

Studies of an Old Man Seated and of Swirling Water

Pen and ink

Two Studies of Horses

Silver-point on orange prepared surface

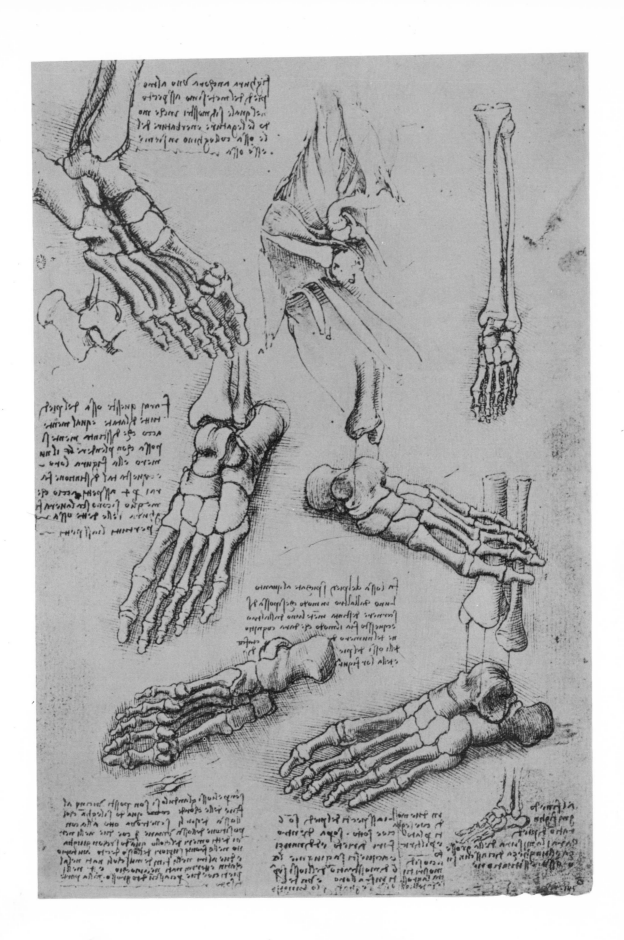

Anatomical Studies of the Foot and Ankle

Pen and ink over faint-black chalk

Studies of Horses, a Cat, and of St. George and the Dragon
Pen and ink

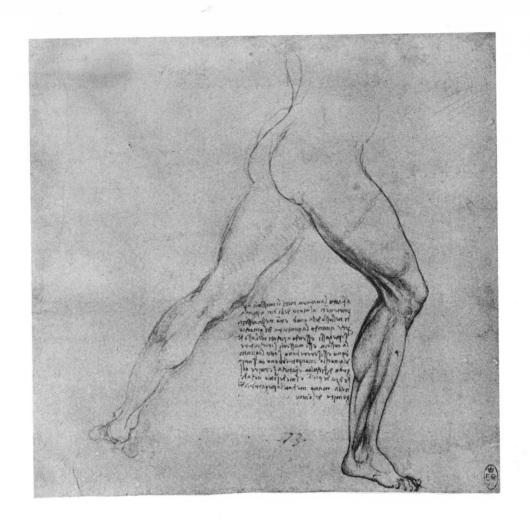

Study of a Man Lunging to the Right
Red chalk on red prepared surface
ROYAL COLLECTION, WINDSOR CASTLE, BERKSHIRE, ENGLAND, COPYRIGHT RESERVED

Study of a Sleeve and Hand
Pen and ink with washes of black
ROYAL COLLECTION, WINDSOR CASTLE, BERKSHIRE, ENGLAND, COPYRIGHT RESERVED

Sheet of Sketches: Madonna Adoring the Child

Pen and bistre on pinkish paper

COURTESY OF THE METROPOLITAN MUSEUM OF ART

NEW YORK CITY, NEW YORK, ROGER FUND 1917

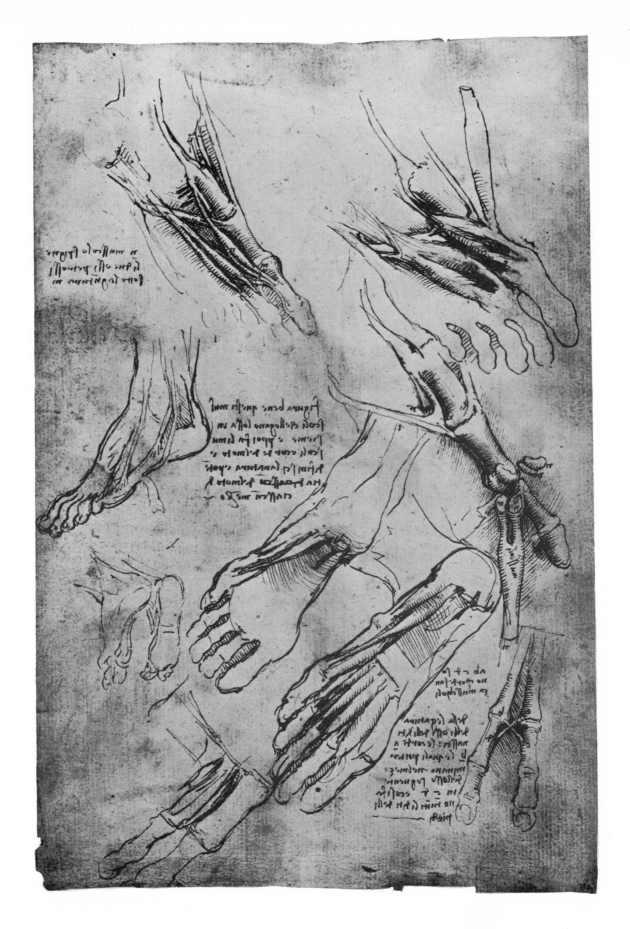

Eight Studies Showing the Structure of the Foot

Pen and ink over faint-black chalk

Anatomical Drawing of Two Skulls in Profile

Pen and ink

Drawing of a Left Leg Showing Bones and Tendons

Pen and ink

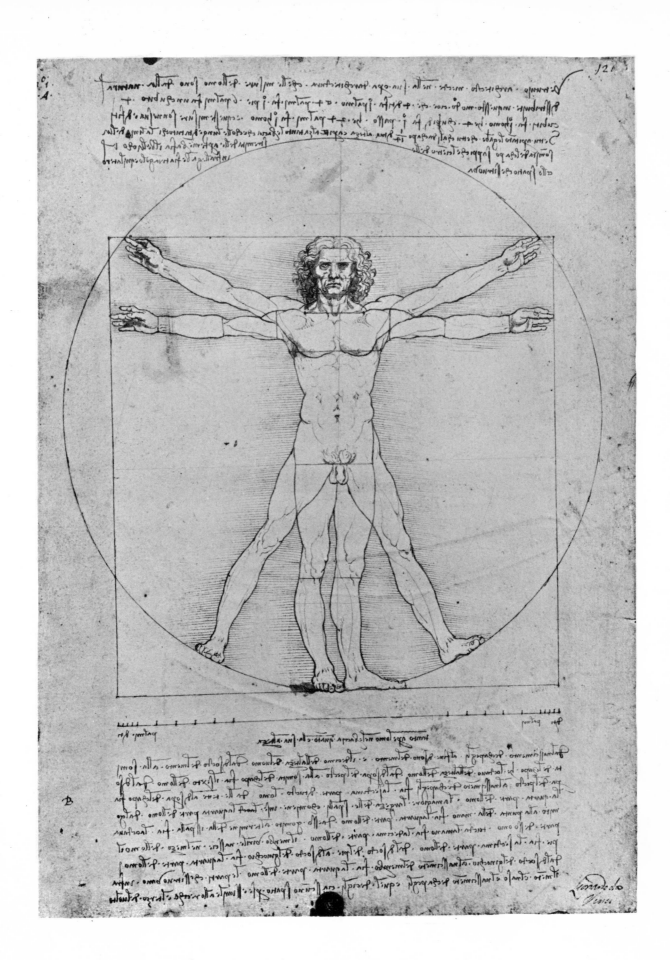

Human Figure in a Circle, Illustrating Proportions

Pen and ink

ACADEMY, VENICE, ITALY

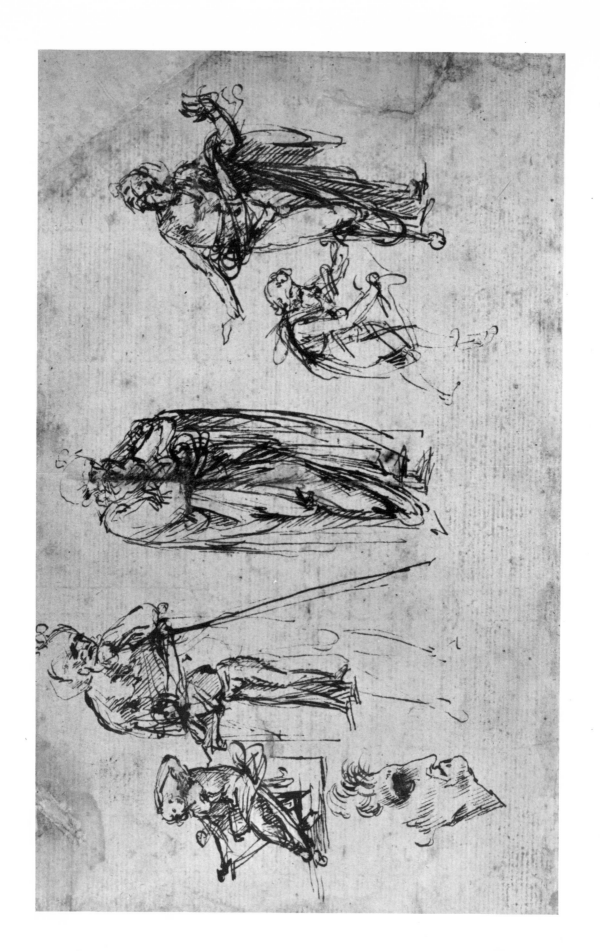

Studies of Single Figures
Pen and ink
BRITISH MUSEUM, LONDON, ENGLAND

Head of an Apostle and Study of Architecture

Red chalk and pen and ink

Three Studies of Horses

Pen and ink over black chalk

Profile of a Girl

Silver-point on pinkish prepared surface

Profiles of Men and Half-Length of a Girl

Pen and ink

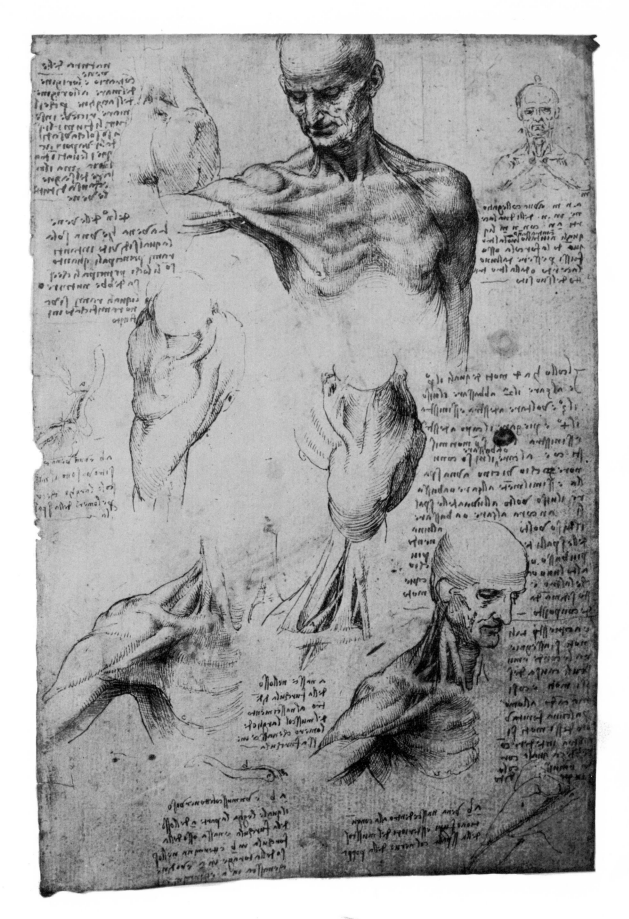

Anatomical Studies of Man's Neck and Shoulders

Pen and ink

A Youth with a Lance
Pen and ink and wash, over black chalk

Man Blowing Trumpet in Another's Ear and Two Figures
Pen and ink over lead-point

Head of a Man Shouting

Red chalk

MUSEUM OF FINE ARTS, BUDAPEST, HUNGARY

Studies of Horses' Heads and Rearing Horse
Pen and ink

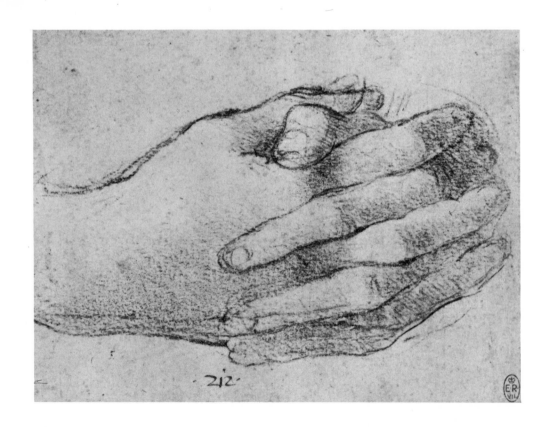

Study of Clasped Hands
Black chalk